Parks and Gardens

Louise and Richard Spilsbury

Heinemann
LIBRARY

www.heinemann.co.uk
Visit our website to find out more information about Heinemann Library books.

To order:
☎ Phone 44 (0) 1865 888066
📄 Send a fax to 44 (0) 1865 314091
💻 Visit the Heinemann Bookshop at www.heinemann.co.uk to browse our catalogue and order online.

First published in Great Britain by Heinemann Library,
Halley Court, Jordan Hill, Oxford OX2 8EJ
a division of Reed Educational and Professional Publishing Ltd.
Heinemann is a registered _____ il Publishing Ltd.

OXFORD MELBOURNE _____ PLANTYRE
GABORONE IBADAN P_____

© Reed Educational an ____
The moral right of the ____

Designed by Celia Floyd
Illustrations by Alan Fr___
Originated by Dot Gradations
Printed in China

ISBN 0 431 03906 2 (hardback)
06 05 04 03 02 01
10 9 8 7 6 5 4 3 2

ISBN 0 431 03913 5 (paperback)
ISBN 978 0 431 03913 8 (paperback)
06
10 9 8 7 6 5 4 3 2

British Library Cataloguing in Publication Data
Spilsbury, Louise
    Parks and gardens. – (Wild Britain)
    1. Garden ecology – Great Britain – Juvenile literature
    2. Garden animals – Great Britain – Juvenile literature
    I. Title II. Spilsbury, Richard
    577.5'54

Acknowledgements

To our own young wildlife enthusiasts, Miles and Harriet.

The Publishers would like to thank the following for permission to reproduce photographs:
Bruce Coleman: p10, Neil McAllister p6, Sir Jeremy Grayson p12, Scott Neilsen p15, Kim Taylor pp21, 23, 26, Jane Burton pp24, 25, George McCarthy p29; Corbis: Kevin Morris p4; FLPA: Maurice Nimmo p19; Garden & Wildlife Matters: p5, Jeremy Hoare p8; Holt: pp7, 28; NHPA: Stephen Dalton p9, Manfred Danegger pp11, 20, Brian Hawkes p16; Oxford Scientific Films: Densey Clyne p14, Harold Taylor p17, David Thompson p18, Mark Hamblin p22, E R Degginger p27; Wildlife Matters p13

Cover photograph reproduced with permission of Images

Our thanks to Andrew Solway for his comments in the preparation of this book.

Every effort has been made to contact copyright holders of any material reproduced in this book. Any omissions will be rectified in subsequent printings if notice is given to the Publisher.

Contents

Any words appearing in the text in bold, **like this**, are explained in the Glossary.

What are parks and gardens?

Plants are sometimes set out in special patterns in parks.

Parks and gardens are areas of grass and other plants that people have made to enjoy. They are usually near the houses that people live in.

Park and garden habitats provide living things with food, water and **shelter**.

A **habitat** is the natural home of a group of plants and animals. In this book we will look at a few of the animals and plants that live, grow and **reproduce** in park and garden habitats.

Types of park and garden

This park is in the middle of a town. It has an area of grass for people to walk on and plants for them to look at.

There are many different places to live in park or garden **habitats**. There can be open, sunny lawns and shaded, damp ground next to fences and hedges.

This garden has not been looked after so all the plants are long and wild.

Some gardens or areas of parkland are left to grow wild. **Insects**, mice, voles and other animals find **shelter** among the grasses and wild flowers.

Changes

Lots of people sit outside when it is sunny, so many animals stay out of sight.

In spring and summer there are many flowers, and trees and shrubs are full of leaves. There is lots of food for animals to eat and thick **shelter** to hide safely in.

Food from a bird table can help birds survive in the winter when there is little food about.

In autumn and winter many of the trees in parks and gardens lose their leaves. There are few flowers and ponds may freeze over. It is hard for animals to find enough food and drink.

Living there

Sometimes people come to parks especially to feed the ducks and geese.

People visit parks and gardens all the time. Gardeners look after the plants and cut the grass. People come to walk and play. Animals that live in parks and gardens have to be able to live near humans.

Cats often catch wild animals like mice to eat.

Birds and other wild animals in parks and gardens also have to cope with living near pets. Pets like cats and dogs can be a danger to small animals.

Trees and hedges

A conker is the **seed** of the horse chestnut tree.

There are many different kinds of trees and shrubs in parks and gardens. Giant horse chestnut trees often grow around the edge of parks.

Small animals find **shelter** inside a privet hedge where it is dark and shady.

Privet hedges are shrubs that are used instead of fences in many parks and gardens. People trim privet to keep it tidy, but more leaves and branches grow back.

Flowering plants

The sweet smell of a rose comes from its colourful petals.

People grow flowering plants, like tulips and roses, in parks and gardens because they look and smell good. **Insects** come to drink their **nectar**.

Dandelions open their yellow petals in the day to soak up the sunlight and close them at night.

Dandelions are flowering plants that grow from **seeds** blown into parks and gardens. Unwanted plants like this are called weeds.

Insects

The **larvae** of the cabbage white butterfly eats cabbages.

Parks and gardens are full of **insects** that feed on the plants, or on other insects. Some are a nuisance to gardeners because they feed on the plants and ruin them.

Ladybirds help gardeners by eating aphids.

Other insects are helpful to gardeners because they eat the insects that damage plants. Ladybirds eat aphids, tiny insects that can destroy roses.

Earthworms and slugs

Worm casts are the piles of soil that have passed through worms' bodies.

Earthworms help plants grow by bringing air into the soil as they burrow under ground. They pass soil through their bodies, taking some of its **nutrients** for their food.

Slugs make slime to help them slide along.

Slugs are a nuisance in the garden because they eat plant leaves. Slugs are like snails without shells. Both move on their flat undersides that act like one big foot.

Sparrows and robins

Sparrows call out a warning at the sign of any danger.

You may see flocks of sparrows gather together on bushes in parks or gardens. They are looking out for each other. While some birds eat, a few keep watch.

Robins are easy to spot with their red breasts.

Birds, like all living things, including us, need water to live. In winter, robins may have to break the ice off pools or fountains to drink the water.

House martins and thrushes

This house martin is feeding its young in the nest with **insects** it has caught in the air.

Birds build nests to lay their eggs in and to **shelter** their young after they **hatch**. House martins build their nests out of mud at the top of houses, under the roof.

This thrush is using its beak to bash snail shells against a stone so it can eat the snail inside.

Birds use beaks and claws to get their food. The thrush uses its strong beak to pull worms out of the soil and to pluck berries from trees. It also eats slugs and snails.

Rats and foxes

Never touch wild rats because they can carry disease.

Rats and mice thrive near people because they can eat almost anything. A rat's sharp teeth can bite through wood and even some metals to get to food.

Foxes may search bins for food at night.

Foxes used to live only in woodlands. Since many woods have been cut down, some foxes now live in parks or gardens in towns. They may eat rats and left-over food.

Squirrels

Grey squirrels use their tails for balance as they run and leap from tree to tree.

You often see squirrels in parks and gardens. They take food from bins and picnic tables as well as eating nuts, **seeds** and **fruits** from the trees.

Squirrels give birth to their young in their dreys.

Squirrels live in nests called dreys. Dreys are made from twigs and lined with soft grass or leaves. In autumn squirrels bury nuts in the ground to eat in winter.

Dangers

Sometimes gardeners cut back trees and shrubs to make them look tidy.

If trees and hedges are cut back in spring and summer it may leave birds' **nests** open to danger. Birds' eggs may then be found and eaten by animals like weasels and foxes.

Dropping litter is bad for wildlife and for people. This woodmouse is stuck in an old bottle.

When people drop litter in parks and gardens it spoils the way they look. Litter may also harm animals, which can choke on plastic bags or get trapped inside empty jars.

Food chains

A food chain shows the link between plants and animals in a **habitat**. There are many different food chains in a park or garden habitat. Here is one example.

The fox eats the thrush or its eggs.

The thrush eats the earthworm.

The earthworm takes in nutrients from the soil.

The artwork on this page is not to scale.

Glossary

fruit the part of a plant or tree that holds its seeds

habitat the natural home of a group of plants and animals

hatch to be born from an egg

insects six-legged minibeasts with bodies divided into three sections: head, thorax (chest) and abdomen (stomach)

larva (plural = **larvae**) stage between hatching from an egg and being an adult in living things whose young look very different to adults. Caterpillars and tadpoles are larvae.

nectar sweet sugary juice in the centre of a flower

nutrients food that gives living things the goodness they need to live and grow

reproduce when plants and animals make young just like themselves

seeds these are made by a plant and released to grow into new plants

shelter somewhere safe to stay, live and have young

Index